INTO AUTUMN

Josefina Beatriz Longoria

Into Autumn
ISBN 978 1 387 62929 9
Designed by Josefina Beatriz Longoria

Dedicated to the happy poets

Table of Contents

Foreword

As a child I did grasp the love of language and chose journalism as my venue. Newspapers are mostly prose. My approach to writing was through ordinary words organized in simple sentence structures. I was more aware of the genres and subgenres of prose than of poetry. In prose, drama can be tragic or comedic, fiction can focus on fantasy, history, mystery, romance, or science fiction.

As writers we need to try on different styles, experiment and leave our comfort zone. The stereotype of the suicidal poet is popular, but maybe that is why poetry is not read as much as self-help literature. People want to find solutions, relax, feel elevated or hopeful. Those who write about contentment, inspiration, or ecstasy are beloved by many. Poets like Rumi and Teresa de Avila are cherished because they speak of the love of God.

We know that narrative is built around conflict. If there is no tension, there is no story. In literature there is an aesthetic preference for the tragic. Scholars are good at criticizing and have developed a taste for drama. In the academic world uplifting literature is foolish.

Prose is straightforward, direct, clear, and practical. It has a purpose and a message. The main emphasis is on what you say. Poetry aims to grasp the sacred, unexplainable, mystic, essence of reality. Poets are freed from the structured narrative of prose, but if this freedom is taken too far, they offer obscurity. The difference between a good poem and a bad one is clarity. Bad poems are difficult to follow because nobody can decipher what they are about.

Sylvia Plath said poetry is a closed fist and prose an open hand. An open hand will slap you, and a closed fist will punch you. Poetry is coded, figurative, has an unpredictable structure, uses repetition and pattern to create a rhythm, and sometimes it rhymes. The focus is on how you say something. Poems can be ornamented, lack purpose, and leave things unsaid. One day, I heard a poem about death, and it shot an arrow to my heart. This poem was more effective than any essay, article, or short story I had read.

We don't have to understand something to be affected by it. This is where poetry comes into play. Prose is explanatory, it lays it out and deconstructs an idea. Poetry is concrete, precise, and raw, it uses language in an unexpected manner. The goal of poems is not to explore facts but to create images and produce an experience for the reader. Poetry is brief, no hay, no fillers, no waste. Directly from my soul to yours.

This book is called *Into Autumn* because these poems are written from the perspective of a certain stage of life. If life were divided into seasons the narrative is from the autumn point of view.

The poems are divided into the four seasons. Spring poems are about childhood: planting, caring, rooting, and waiting. Summer poems are about becoming an adult: creating, producing, reproducing, and growing. Autumn poems are about reaching maturity: trimming, harvesting, organizing, and resting. Winter poems are about hibernation: preparing to go dormant and rebirth.

ABOUT THE AUTHOR

Josefina Beatriz Longoria has been an author, editorial columnist, correspondent, radio, and television commentator. She earned her Bachelor of Arts in Communication and Master of Arts in Organizational Development, from Universidad de Monterrey, Mexico. In addition, she earned a second Master of Arts in Creative Writing from Our Lady of the Lake University in San Antonio, Texas.

She graduated from The Masters School in Dobbs Ferry New York, attended a dance workshop at Harvard University and studied French Civilization at La Sorbonne. She wrote a film script, authored "The Journalist Writer" and through her first book *Retratos de Una Burguesia* (1996) was a chosen author for the anthology *A traves de los Ojos de Ella (1999.* Josefina's editorial contributions span several years for various Mexican newspapers.

She self-published her memoir *Uproot* (2018) and *Enjoy: How to Create a Positive Narrative (2021.)* The book *Into Autumn* is a selection of poems written from 2016 to 2022.

SPRING

A SPECIAL PLACE

Old garage dance studio,
Girls running up the stairs
Black leotards, pink tights, leg warmers

Round windows doubled in mirrors
Music commands, hands on bars, leg in the air
Coccyx and pelvis together, vertebrae aligned

Ballet slippers brushing wood floor
Cross the room, turn, twirl, focus
Chin up, elbows high, point your toes

"Teacher, teacher, look at me, only me"

New dance studio, tall ceiling, spacious parking
Woman paying for a single class
Colored leotards, neon shorts

Obedient girls, generation after generation
My reflection shows a full-grown woman
No magic for adults, no power for teachers

"Look girls, the teacher lost her halo"

FAVORITE THINGS

3	A good long and restful nap
6	To play in a bubble bath with a rubber ducky
9	Birthday party, balloons, gifts, and candy
12	Splashing, jumping in the trampoline
15	Jogging, training, competing for the finish line
18	Classes, studying, exams to stand on podium
21	Music, drinking and dancing the night away
24	Flirting, kissing, hugging and foreplay
27	Courting, searching, ring and wedding
30	Pregnancy test, crib, baby, and a baptism
33	A good long and restful nap with the baby
36	Preparing bubble bath and the rubber ducky
39	Organizing birthday party with balloons
42	Sitting down while they splash and jump
45	Driving them from practice to practice
48	Watch them graduate on the podium
51	Read, write, paint, travel, rest
54	A hot summer splashing in the ocean
57	A sunny afternoon outside gardening
60	Birthday party with balloons, gifts, and candy
63	A bubble bath with jazz in the background
66	Long restful nap after the grandchildren leave

SHARING
To my friends

You mother me and explain myself to me
Your wisdom resolves puzzles

You identify plot and characters
You find solutions and give me hope

We share, we wonder, we dream

How irrational are we?
It does not matter as longs as we laugh

You have problems of the married life
I have problems of the divorced life

We walk together, side by side, each on her journey
We investigate our lives on the phone

We share, we wonder, we dream

SKEIN

In the morning, I get a new hank of yarn
Thoughts are neatly organized in a skein

I open my eyes and pull out the first strand
It is bright and thin like a ray of sunshine
Simple and clear: "I am here, I am alive, I can breathe"

Then comes the twist, the loop
What happened last night? Did you mess things up?
"You are an idiot and should have not said that"

The yarn is entangled and linked, just breathe
"It made sense at the time, an appropriate reply"
The string is pulled, the knot undone

Throughout the day cords are threaded and jammed
Thoughts mesh building a maze, a complex labyrinth
Useless to pretend being a spider knitting a web

At night, I am the fly trapped in the rummage of reason
Tomorrow, the day will begin with one strand again

STAY

Today I think about tomorrow looking back to today
Jump forward to the future and back to the past
Will days to come be better or worse?
Stay in the present like a dog waiting for a bone

Stay, stay, stay.

Chase for a better future while stuck in the present
Anticipation is making me late
Am I where I am supposed to be?
Stay in the present like a cat waiting for a fish

Stay, stay, stay.

This moment was planned yesterday
These perfect words have been rehearsed
No improvisation only choreographed anticipation
Enjoying now because these are the good old days
Stay in the present like a horse waiting for a carrot

Stay, stay, stay.

COLD WATER GLASS

Pulled away from a shelf
Washed, dried, and reused
You come and go in trays
One of many, made in a factory

You come and go ignored
Waiters bring you without asking
Round, short, full, and sweaty
Shiny, cold, water container

Translucent mirror reflecting light and darkness
You stand alone with your three shadows
Now you are unique, you crush my thirst
I hold you, kiss you and leave you

FAST CAR

Left my son in college "Take care honey"
Driving alone, toll Road,
open highway, speed limit 85
Bright sun, blue sky, clouds chasing me

Tire legs roll on pavement,
wheel arms steer the car
Laser eyes see ahead,
my body inside a metal bullet

No people, cities, towns
No cars, traffic, signs, fearless
I own the horizon

Loud music, young like when I first drove a fast car
Present, here, and now, driving like it is Formula 1
Yellow alert blinks low fuel

No people, cities, towns
No cars, traffic, signs, fearful
No fucken gas stations

LIVE MUSIC

Sung poetry, shared lyrics
Enthralled, smitten, enchanted

Words speak of love and sunshine
We hear we are going to change the world

This band is other bands
This singer is just another hunk

We sing along and become young, it's our song
Soundwaves plug us to good old days

We rock and sway now
We rocked and swayed then

WAITING TO PAIR

You lie in bed thinking of someone
Me too
You wonder when the person will show up
Me too
You go out looking for the one
Me too
You pump iron and squat to be ready
Me too

Did he like me?
Does he call? Do I call?
How many days do I wait?
Will he really call?

Waiting to share
Waiting to stare
Waiting to pair

Me into we, I into us, his and hers
From take out, to cooking and make out

WHERE I LIVE

My house is where I eat and sleep
It is a clean space, a shrine of peace
Come in and leave your bitterness out

My body is my worldly residence
Made of fruits, vegetables, nuts, and grains
We can break bread, but it must be multigrain

My soul lives in my chest
Trained by priests and nuns
We can meditate and pray together

My home is in my mind
Filled with ideas, words, and dreams
Your free key is eloquence and wit

My identity resides with my friends
Our connection is art and beauty
Write, paint or dance and join us

PAIN AND JOY

Pain is pain
Nobody owns it
Pain is felt by everybody
Blondes, redheads, and brunettes
Pain is felt from top to bottom
Painful millionaires, painful homeless
Pain is felt in solitude or multitude
alone in bed or in line at the market
Pain is in your brain, stomach, and heart
Losing someone at the hospital or battlefield

Joy is joy
It does not belong to anybody
Joy is felt by everybody
Asians, Jews, Hispanics
Joy is felt in any place
Joyful ghettos and joyful gated communities
Joy is in your body or another body
Eating hot soup or making a baby at night
Joy is in the sparkle of your child's eyes,
the pressed smile between your cheeks

TODAY

It is always today
It is always now
It is always here
What is this moment?
What is this present?

It escapes me while remembering or planning
It escapes me while sad for past or fearful for future
Today was tomorrow just yesterday
Today will be yesterday only tomorrow
What is today? This morning, afternoon, or evening?

The sun is shining now
The fog of sadness is behind me
The clouds of fear are ahead of me
The present glows and radiates around me
I stand on the present

I am an acrobat on a thin tightrope
Step by step, foot by foot, walking on now
My eyes are not filming the present
My eyes are projecting my light into the present
Joy is coming from a sacred space inside

SUMMER

LIMERENT SONNET
(Limerence: the state of being infatuated or obsessed
with another person)

Limerent from teenage years to middle age
Eighteen-month hormonal chemical spell
Romantic nostalgia in every stage
Want to love and be loved to show and tell

Desire in throat, heart, stomach covered
Lust from illusions, dreams, and fantasy
Inertia to smell, touch, taste, the other
Arms legs embrace open to ecstasy

Animal instinct fornicate driven
Possession, obsession, want, and desire
Species survival between legs hidden
Romance disguised in costume and attire

Pretend to be civilized when we meet
Pretend we are well mannered sexy meat

SED-USED

Wanting to want, desire of desire
Fantasy, vanity, surrender, power

No facts, no routine, no family
No feelings, no intimacy, no reality

Agile predator choosing prey
Stalking before attack

Seduction through flattery
Compliments melt the will

Want to see more, show more
Quid pro quo

From electric to magnetic
Simmer the senses to defeat the body

Everything is about sex,
But sex is about power

BARITONE

Poised Adonis enters scene
Seductor with low baritone voice
Only male with blond hair
Enough resemblance to stare

Protagonists looking for each other
Who can play his counterpart?
Skin hungry for playacting
Young flesh for performing

Make me feel I am the only one
You are the only one
Fantasy shattered with vanity
Spotlight is only on you

From top balcony it is an audition
Not enough talent for this rendition
The baritone leaves empty handed
Flirting backstage not to be stranded

CATCH ON MATCH

Browsing over an ocean of men
fake smiles, honest smiles

Car selfie, bathroom selfie, gym selfie
Hiking selfie, scuba selfie, motorbike selfie

Tattoos, t-shirts, blazers, and ties
Hiding behind glasses, showing off biceps

A cruel binary decision: yes or no
Who is a player? Who will be played?

You like beaches and mountains, jeans, and tuxedos?
This does not help, tell me what you love

Transactional interaction, cold interviews
Defenses up, caution up, distrust up

"What is a woman like you doing here?"
That's right! What the hell am I doing here?

TRAINING BOYFRIEND

I don't miss your torn hat, curly hair, or sad eyes
I don't miss your cat, dirty truck or undecorated flat
I don't miss our free dates walking in public parks

I don't miss your tank tops, bright socks, or incense
I don't miss your tribal traditions or clan superiority
I don't miss our bike rides beyond the tracks

I don't miss your cowboy legs or fungus on your toe
I don't miss your music, hammock, or backyard
I don't miss your thighs, shoulders, or forearms

Then why am I still thinking about you?

Because you saved me a little

HAVE AND HAVE NOTS

The has-beens and their stories
The up-and-coming and their plans

Some had, others have
Some went, others are going

Some are the children of
Others are the parents of

Some are the descendants
Others are the ascendants

Some have class for sale
Others are buying it

Endless communion of pretenses
Live, learn, have, and let go

Wash rinse repeat wash rinse repeat
From nothing to everything to nothing

LADIES WHO LUNCH

Ladies finding purpose in themed parties
Attire and costume to find allies

Housekeeping is the meaning of life
A good home the goal of married life

Buying unique objects to build reputation
Prestige by high-end brand association

Dressing rooms to make over
Embroidered pillows to switch over

The mirror a portal to introverts
The living room for social extroverts

What are we doing?
Who are we trying to impress?

RIGHTEOUS DIVORCEE

"I don't have to worry about a thing"
Your trembling hand is evidence of antidepressants

"My lawyers got me all I wanted"
And yet your fourteen-dollar shoes are inside budget

"If their father remarries it will affect them, not me"
A selfish smile in sostenuto

"I am having the best sex of my life!"
Long nails, high heels, cleavage scream available

"I rented a house and he stayed with me"
You are a sugar Mama and don't know it

"I do not have a job, but I am all set"
Life is long and any money can be spent

"He left for a woman half my age"
The victim's script encore

"He lives in sin and is a social outcast"
I see why he left

LINKS

Included with the locals, import no MORE
MORE friends, more acquaintances, more OPTIONS
OPTIONS for light entertainment and NETWORK
NETWORK that expands and contracts, in and OUT

OUT and about, celebrating an American HOLIDAY
HOLIDAY announcing the end of the SUMMER
SUMMER that was filled with WORKSHOPS
WORKSHOPS for writing, eating, and BREATHING

BREATHING that gets me high on OXYGEN
OXYGEN that expands my lungs and gives ENERGY
ENERGY that comes up and out of my BODY
BODY as an ally that is under my CONTROL

CONTROL out of my hands, I meet another LINK
LINK to link builds connections that MULTIPLY
MULTIPLY ripples that grow and EXPAND
EXPAND my identity in a new community

THE EVE

Absurd, irrational expectations
Try harder, try better, try more
Guests are late, meat is dry, music is loud
Don't bring that up! Change the subject, just be quiet
Today happiness is mandatory

Cheer and joy on demand, right now!
You had a bad year? Suck it up, pretend it was good

Dress up, clean up, show up
Be merry and bright
Real tree, real love, real family
Real smothering togetherness

Velvet costume, pearls, heels
Gifts, wrappings, ribbons
A night to prepare us for the cold winter ahead

Christmas is not just for children
I am Santa and this is exhausting!
Can I get another drink please?

TOMORROW

The future will be brighter, better, bountiful
The future is forward, ahead, beyond
There is a light at the end of the tunnel
Tomorrow is one day away
We will fix it, improve it, upgrade it
We will stop smoking, drinking, and eating sugar
We will pray and meditate, tomorrow
That gives us one more day, it is never tomorrow
The thrill of anticipating the future
The dopamine of planning for better days to come
The promise of a brighter time, but never today
Tomorrow never comes

Children are afraid of life
One day things change
Adults are afraid of death

The past was brighter, better, bountiful
The past was full, fun, and filled with expectations
We came out of the tunnel and there was another
Tomorrow is getting closer
A truth in the morning is a lie in the afternoon
Clothes worn in spring don't cover us in autumn
We stop living in the future because it is here
What we want to improve or fix, must be done today

PRIVATE TO PUBLIC

A person has a couch
A couple has a bench
Siblings have the den
Families dine around a table

Fish swim in their tanks
Cats have the sunny spot
Dogs run in the backyard
Birds nest on tree branches

Bicycles ride on sidewalks
Cars drive on streets
Neighbors meet in parks
Communities gather in plazas

Paris has Champs-Elysees
New York has Central Park
Mexico City has the Zocalo
San Antonio has Hemisfair

Hemisfair is our past
Hemisfair is our future

AUTUMN

WORDS

Our alphabet, twenty-six letters
Infinite combinations of syllables
From dictionary to encyclopedia
The world in alphabetical order

Spoken words, from mouth to ear
Written words, from hand to eye

Pointing to things, places, and people
Expressing sensations, thoughts, and feelings

Small and big words that have small meanings
Small and big words that have big meanings

A word is a command, password, or signal
It can be negative, positive, or neutral

Words are symbols of symbols
A word that points to a thing
A thing that points to an idea
My words are yours now

DIVORCE IS HERE

A heavy gray lead blanket
Lying in bed afraid of you

An implacable destroyer
big reset, big unroot, big restart

Then enormous waves like a tsunami
Now a gentle tide that touches my ankles

Twenty years my diamond ring shielded me
Twenty years hiding behind my man protected me
Twenty years of being afraid of you taking me

Marriage was a bliss, then a crowd, then a cage
Divorce you are here to carry me into a new stage

JUST LEAVE

You thrive among corporations
A bright star in safari conventions
Addicted to your bow and arrow
The thrill of the kill fills your tomorrow

While in VIP lounge and mimosa for breakfast
At home we tended to the autistic blast

Explosive tantrums, broken bowls,
Broken windows, broken walls

Sleepless night and early morning
pure love through endless yawning

You are free, just leave already,
Now family of three, tight and steady

YOU MISSED IT

Even when you were there you were missing
At the hospital with a newborn, plugged into WIFI
At confirmation, texting when holy spirit came
At the beach, you missed sand, water, and ice cream

You missed jumping or baking banana nut bread
We bonded pushing strollers and driving to school

I taught them to eat, dress, write, read, talk, listen
I taught them to say please, thank you and grace
I even taught our son to check and fill his tires

Creating the perfect fund or answering one last call
You missed it all

IT WOULD PASS

We were quiet on Saturdays
Green tea at 5am
Twenty-one allergy morning sneezes
Crumbled Kleenex were your droppings

You had no peace, hyperactive mind
Cold, distant, busy, apart

Children demanding attention
Video games, toys, puzzles, television

Cleaning, cooking, picking up
Cleaning, cooking, picking up

Wishing it would pass
It did

LETTING GO
To my son David

Let go, you go, we go
A smile, a kiss, a hug
Good morning, good night
A thousand and one nights

You are mine I am yours forever
You have your journey
You are my teacher and blessed me
You need to go now and bless others

I let you go my cherub
You are my twinkle star
I am your island
you are my continent

You are the answered prayer I did not know I made
You transformed me, not just for you but for others
You chose me, what did you see in me?
You master, you guru, you angel

Go and make a difference
I will do the same

MOM WAS MY NAME
For my son Tomas

Images of my boy are present in my mind
Now that boy is a foot taller than me
He is still mine, but a lot less mine
Seeing him as a man fills me with pride

We are not as close as we were, detached
We are in different cities, leading separate lives

You defend your adulthood and keep your distance
Your college keeps you busy building a future life

Your girlfriend is your sunshine
You are my sunshine forever
Give me one hug, just one more please
It is still not easy to let go

Your independence was always the goal
Now, your room at home is tidy and clean
There is less laundry, and the kitchen is pristine
There was a time when Mom was my name all day

THESE BOYS

My boys are here
The dog barks

TV on, kitchen smells like stew
Not a house, now a home

Objects come to life
These boys make sense of it all

My masterpiece, my legacy
Where I lay it all out

Holidays are small at home
I am Santa and the Easter bunny

No man required in the kitchen
Superpowers of the homemaker

My kindness and care are replaceable
The value of what I built is sustainable

HERE I AM

Not out there but here
Not others, but me
No distraction but attraction

I am on the right path
I am stepping in
I am beating strong

Walking on sunshine
Walking on moonlight
Walking on blood line

Too much of them? For sure
Too much of you? Depends
Too much of me? Impossible

HARVEST

Brushing, sweeping, wiping, washing
Reappropriate every corner

Clean up and throw out
History in objects that hold memories

Each house has an era
Objects outlive us, stare at us

No daydreaming, no illusions
No soulmate, no prince, no knight

I am enough, I am yin and yang
Whole, centered, balanced, content

Warrior with my own shining armor
Harvest now, settle down later

BASEMENT

Our basements hide different shadows
Our living rooms show bright and happy things
I walk into bedrooms, kitchen, and peek into closets
You hang out in the den, dining room and garage
We do not go near the underworld
One day, we mention that hidden space below
Your eyes look away, I get a nervous laugh
We change the subject to green gardens
We get busy to excuse ourselves for not decluttering
I cook, eat, or drink, while you shop, clean, or read
Distress follows us to the spa, the bar, and the plane
We complain about soreness, aches, and pains
You brag about new sheets, comforter, and pillows
I plan to replace carpets, tiles, and wallpaper
Finally, you say: "We should clean the basement"
We are relieved, exhale and cry while we hug
We commit to dive deep down and organize
Down the steps is an ocean of what was
This flood of emotions drips down eyes and nose
Ripples of sadness turn into waves of grief
Clouds of fear announce the thunder of anger
The drizzle of loss turns into a storm of betrayal
Despair sinks into the depths of loneliness
The angst of drowning makes anxiety heavy
Doubt pulls further down, and guilt asphyxiates
At the bottom there it is, the stillness

WHAT IS NEXT?

What is next? Something?
Anything? Everything?

A clean slate, reset
Another beginning
On your marks, get set, go!

No attachments, nothing pending
My life starts now
No need to please anybody

In control
In command
At the wheel

I am the pilot
I am the chief
I am the boss

The best time is now
Clean basement, clean closet, clean attic
Open arms to embrace what is next

WINTER

NIGHT SKY

A short drive away city reflection behind
Cooler, darker, quieter, another rhythm
Electricity fades, galaxies appear above
Off the grid, plug into another power

Shy creatures sneak out
Wilderness is timeless
Hills, trees, and bushes have no age
Crickets and cicadas live, die, and live again

The space is immense, vast, and abundant
Twinkling stars are needles piercing the sky
We poke infinity and wish upon a wink of light

FOUR O'CLOCK

4 pm energy drops, temperature drops
with twilight come shadows and decline
the time of fairies and fireflies ends with dusk
flowers close their petals
light diminishes, darkness grows
my body weakens
my mind drifts into the dream world
dreams turn into nightmares
tossing and turning

4 am appointment with demons
problems grow, solutions leave
obscurity smothers, night suffocates
then the first bird tweet announces dawn
shadows dissolve, sunrays extend
visibility is restored, morning expands

I am strong as I rise with the sun

CONTAGION
To my poetry teacher Octavio Quintanilla

Did he bring it from Mexico or was it already here?
Does he spread it with a glance or his voice?

I was infected on a winter night
The right words and the pest entered through my ears

There was no sneeze, cough, or headache
Is it a cardiac condition or a stomach bug?

Was it infection or medication?
Is this an illness or a cure?

Eyes can see the clouds move
Ears can hear the grass grow

Stay away from him! Get quarantined!
This could be lethal or a pass to eternity

Stop reading! This is contagious!
These words are proof of my malady

INWARD BOUND

Four months that feel like four years
The same day over and over

Days are longer, weeks are shorter
Frozen between yesterday and tomorrow

No sports, fashion, concerts or shows
No hugs, kisses, or handshakes

Island, social distance, island
Morning walks to wave at others

No gatherings, reunions, or cocktails
No touching or closeness

Hiding our faces
Self-contained units

The big pause
Pandemic inward bound

ANTIDOTE

Sin is the superior judge
It perpetuates the daily subtraction

Sin is the dark lens that obscures
Guilt that oppresses the heart

Sin is the indigestible poison
Venom that intoxicates the mind

Sin is the joy killer
Pesticide for flowers

Sin is a daily hara-kiri
The cruel island of shame

Forgiveness is the antidote
Forgiveness is the master key
Forgiveness is the way out of the nightmare

LIFE STILL IS

Health, sickness, health, sickness
Love, loneliness, love, loneliness
Abundance, lack, abundance, lack
The roller coaster of life

Sometimes we have health, love, and money
Sometimes we have sickness, loneliness, and lack
Sometimes we have inner peace

With each reset we bounce back higher
With each reboot we rebound faster
With each restart we leap back stronger

We leave our comfort, come back improved
We leave the familiar, come back enhanced
We leave the known, come back changed

Life still is a surprise
Life still is an adventure
Life still is a gift

Children look ahead to the future
Elders look back to the past
Life still is now, only right now

BIG C

Sneaky invisible killer
It lurks, prowls and hunts
Where does it come from?
Outside or inside?

It is an enemy cell gone wild, gone bad
It is a growth, a mass, a lump, a bump
It is me against me? How can that be?

Where did your big C go?
Your breast, colon, or lung?
Did you feel it? Did you kill it?
Does it linger in blood, bones, or lymph nodes?

Big C, you are not as big as you think

You are just a deep hurt unattended
You are just a longstanding resentment
You are just a shameful secret fermented

Who knew threat could bring such peace?
Who knew death could make us live?

While there is breath, life wins

SMALL LOVE
To Luis

First time you saw me I was six
Walking down the stairs in Mom's heels

Later in life we saw each other
You were the cool older guy

You were all I wanted
I was all you wanted

Then you broke my heart once
Then you broke my heart twice

My first kiss, my first love
My first illusion, my first disillusion

I lived a good life, you did not
Now you are gone

I see more, I see better, I see beyond
Our hug in the elevator was our last bond

Your charm was enough to enthrall
But your love was always small

POCKET WATCH

Watch the watch mark time
Time watches us age
We watch time in our wrinkles
Time interrupts our daily lives

Watch days turn into years
Time ticks, tic-toc-tic-toc
Watch the hands go around and around
Time is the shadow that follows life

How dare you be finite? Why push us to death?
You deceive us? Do you come and go? You just go
I changed my skin from a girl to a woman
I still breathe, he exhaled

Three years ago, I was married
Three years ago, he was alive

We dissolve
We fade into infinity
We are stardust

THIS BODY
To my father

For eighty-six years this was your body
Since 1933 you were a strong man

Your body jogged before it was fashionable
Your body swam breaking the ocean waves
Your body dived from the highest board
Your body hiked mountains in record time

You hugged me when I was a girl
I hugged you when you were an old man

This body exhaled
This body is pale
This body has no soul
This body is a shed skin

This body was you, now it is not
Where did you go?

WITHOUT U
(Lipogram without the letter I)

You are gone, not here, not now, not ever
You are absent, faded, transformed

We look for new forms to relate
We connect through a new network

You were mortal, now you are dead
You were a body, now you are a soul

We were young, now we are old
We were your toddlers, now we are parents

Your memory stays on photographs
Your proof on album pages

We are apart, we mourn alone
We create closure through what is grown

BECOME AGAIN

There is a void, a blackhole, an empty space
My universe is expanding and contracting
I am at the end of my cold dark winter
Earlier and brighter dawns are coming

Sprouting, blooming, blossoming? Not yet
Time for rooting quietly underground
More sunlight, more water, more air
Things are not ready, they are becoming

Wind blows the last dead leaves
Crossing the valley of the fallen
We die a little to be born again
A train slides through the city at night

Creating with what is already here
Nothing is completely new
Healed wounds turn into fallen scabs
Recreate, grow, and become again

·